D1017033

GREAT HISPANIC AND LATINO AMERICANS

Ellen Ochoa

by Christine Juarez

CAPSTONE PRESS
a capstone imprint

Pebble Books are published by Capstone Press,
1710 Roe Crest Drive, North Mankato, Minnesota 56003
www.mycapstone.com

Library of Congress Cataloging-in-Publication Data
Names: Juarez, Christine, 1976– author.
Title: Ellen Ochoa / by Christine Juarez.
Description: North Mankato, Minnesota : Capstone Press, [2017] | Series: Pebble
books. Great Hispanic and Latino Americans. | Audience: Ages 4–8. |
Audience: K to grade 3. | Includes bibliographical references and index.
Identifiers: LCCN 2016003662| ISBN 9781515718888 (library binding) | ISBN
9781515718994 (pbk.) | ISBN 9781515719199 (eBook pdf) Subjects: LCSH: Ochoa,
Ellen—Juvenile literature. | Women astronauts—United States—Biography—
Juvenile literature. | Astronauts—United States—Biography—Juvenile literature.
| Women scientists—United States—Biography—Juvenile literature. | Hispanic
American women—Biography—Juvenile literature.
Classification: LCC TL789.85.O25 J83 2017 | DDC 629.450092—dc23
LC record available at http://lccn.loc.gov/2016003662

Note to Parents and Teachers

The Great Hispanic and Latino Americans series supports national
curriculum standards for social studies related to people, places,
and culture. This book describes and illustrates Ellen Ochoa.
The images support early readers in understanding the text. The
repetition of words and phrases helps early readers learn new
words. This book also introduces early readers to subject-specific
vocabulary words, which are defined in the Glossary section. Early
readers may need assistance to read some words and to use the
Table of Contents, Glossary, Read More, Internet Sites, and Index
sections of the book.

Printed in the United States of America in North Mankato, Minnesota.
042017 010473R

Table of Contents

Ellen as a child

1958
born

About Ellen

Ellen Ochoa is an inventor
and an astronaut. She was
the first Hispanic woman
to go into space. Ellen was
born May 10, 1958,
in Los Angeles, California.

x

1958
born

As a child, Ellen was curious.

From her parents, Ellen learned

that school was important.

Ellen was a good student.

She enjoyed math, science,

and music.

Ellen earned two degrees at Stanford.

1958
born

1980
graduates from
San Diego State
University

8

Scientist and Inventor

After high school, Ellen went

to San Diego State University.

She studied physics.

Ellen graduated in 1980.

Then she studied electrical

engineering at Stanford University.

1958
born

1980
graduates from
San Diego State
University

After school, Ellen worked

at science research centers.

As a scientist, she made

three inventions. Her inventions

help computers "see" images.

Ellen during astronaut training

1958
born

1980
graduates from
San Diego State
University

1990
enters
astronaut
training

Astronaut Ochoa

Ellen had another big goal.

She wanted to go into space.

Ellen applied to NASA's

astronaut program.

In 1990 Ellen entered

astronaut training. Ellen's first

space flight was in 1993.

1993
first space
flight

Ellen played her flute during her first space flight.

1958
born

1980
graduates from San Diego State University

1990
enters astronaut training

14

In space, Ellen and her crew
studied how the sun affects
earth's atmosphere.
Ellen also ran a robotic arm.
She went on three more
space missions. Ellen spent
nearly 1,000 hours in space.

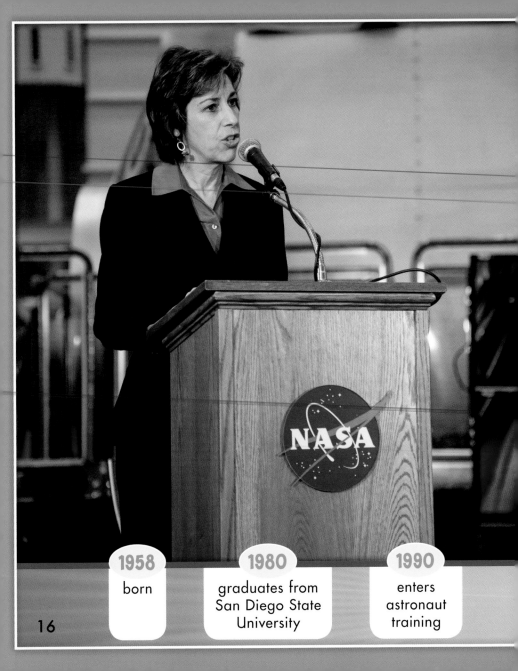

1958
born

1980
graduates from
San Diego State
University

1990
enters
astronaut
training

Ellen's Life Today

Ellen still works for NASA.

She became the director

of the Johnson Space Center

in 2012. The space center is

home to mission control.

1993
first space
flight

2012
becomes the director
of the Johnson
Space Center

1958	1980	1990
born	graduates from San Diego State University	enters astronaut training

Ellen continues to speak about her time being an astronaut. Ellen especially enjoys speaking to students. Four schools in the United States have been named after her.

1993
first space
flight

2012
becomes the director
of the Johnson
Space Center

1958
born

1980
graduates from
San Diego State
University

1990
enters
astronaut
training

By becoming an astronaut,
Ellen also became a role model.
She has achieved many
of her goals. Ellen wants
to help others achieve
their goals too.

1993
first space
flight

2012
becomes the director
of the Johnson
Space Center

Glossary

achieve—to reach a level or a goal after putting in a great deal of effort

atmosphere—the mixture of gases that surrounds some planets and moons

graduate—to finish all the classes required at a school

Hispanic—a person of Mexican, South American, or other Spanish-speaking background

mission control—the group of people on earth that helps direct the astronauts in space

physics—the science that deals with matter and energy; physics includes the study of light, heat, sound, electricity, motion, and force

robotic arm—a machine that reaches outside of the spacecraft to do certain jobs in space

train—to prepare for something by learning and practicing new skills

Read More

Keedle, Jayne. *Ellen Ochoa.* People We Should Know. Pleasantville, N.Y.: Gareth Stevens Pub., 2009.

McAneney, Caitie. *Women in Space.* Women Groundbreakers. New York: PowerKids Press, 2016.

Wooster, Patricia. *An Illustrated Timeline of Space Exploration.* Visual Timelines in History. North Mankato, Minn.: Picture Window Books, 2012.

Internet Sites

FactHound offers a safe, fun way to find Internet sites related to this book. All of the sites on FactHound have been researched by our staff.

Here's all you do:

Visit *www.facthound.com*

Type in this code: 9781515718888

Super-cool stuff! Check out projects, games and lots more at **www.capstonekids.com**

Index

Editorial Credits

Erika L. Shores, editor; Charmaine Whitman, designer;
Kelly Garvin, media researcher; Tori Abraham, production specialist

Photo Credits

AP Images/Kai-Huei Yau, Tri-City Herald, 18; NASA: Johnson Space Center, cover, 1,
12, 14, 20, Kennedy Space Center/Robert Markowitz, 16; Photo courtesy of Dr. Ellen
Ochoa, 4, 6, 8; Photo courtesy of Sandia National Laboratories, 10
Artistic Elements: Shutterstock: Eliks, nalinn, tuulijumala